CONTENTS

ABOUT THE AUTHOR

Kenneth P. Kosier works as a school psychologist in the Madison, Wisconsin school district. He obtained his doctorate degree in educational psychology at the University of Wisconsin. In addition to serving a number of elementary and secondary schools over the last 32 years, he has served as program evaluator for the Madison District and for the Wisconsin State Department of Public Instruction. During this time, the University of Wisconsin and the Southwest Wisconsin Education Organization sponsored Kosier to lecture and conduct workshops on student discipline throughout the Midwest. Currently, he practices school psychology full time at Aldo Leopold Elementary School in Madison.

CONTRIBUTING TEACHERS

Mike Balk
Mary Billings
Cheryl Callin
Catherine Clemons
Karen Cook
Susan Cutler
Carol Dickerson
Teri Downing
Berlinder Fry
Frances Gilmore
Rebecca Gipson
Fritz Hammer
Susan Hammer
Thomas Hanley
Michael Holba
Pamela Holland-Mills
Sue Human
Jeff Jenning
Christine Jones
Sandra Kaufman-Harris
Andrea Knutson
Martha Kronholm
Sharon Kusch
Donna Lamphiear
Wendy Martin
Beth McLimans
Richard Lenz
Bonnie Lesperance
Kathleen Otto
Paula Peterson
Carol Pineo
Carol Polipnick
Cathleen Powers
Dottie Priddy
Janet L. Rhodes
Thelma Mae Robinson
Mary Schliem
Betty Shellswick
Nancy Skarich
Karen Sobczyk
Tim Somers
Dave Spitzer
Lee-Ann W. Stephens
Lori Stepping
Melissa Stratton
Jill Searchy Taylor
Kathleen Thompson
Maude Turner

THE DISCIPLINE CHECKLIST

Advice from 60 Successful Elementary Teachers

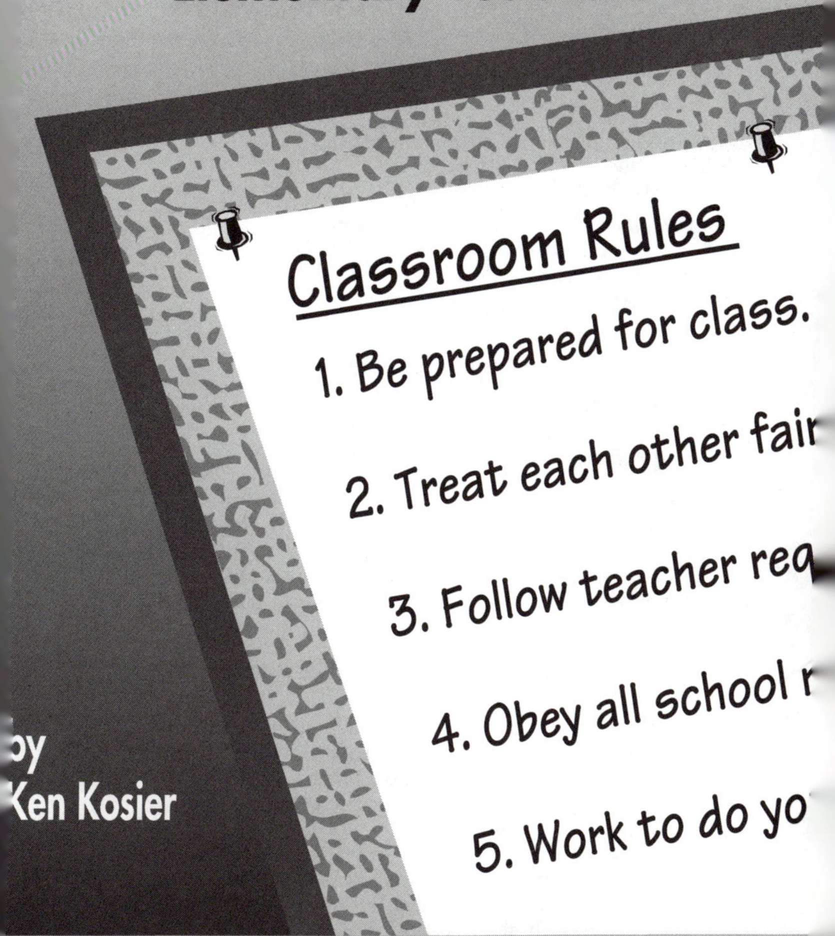

by
Ken Kosier

NEA CHECKLIST SERIES
AN NEA PROFESSIONAL LIBRARY PUBLICATION

ADVISORY PANEL

Printing History:
First Printing: July 1998
Second Printing: June 2000

Note: The opinions expressed in this publication should not be construed as representing the policy or position of the National Education Association. Materials published by the NEA Professional Library are intended to be discussion documents for educators who are concerned with specialized interests of the profession.

Library of Congress Cataloging-in-Publication Data

Kosier, Ken
The discipline checklist: advice from 60 successful elementary teachers / by Ken Kosier.
p. cm. — (NEA checklist series)
Includes bibliographical references.
ISBN 0-8106-2160-6 (pbk.)
1. School discipline—United States. 2. Problem children—Education—United States. 3. Motivation in education—United States. I. Title. II. Title: Preparing for today's difficult students. III. Series.
LB3012.2.K67 1998
371.5'0973—DC21 97-49863
CIP

14

INTRODUCTION

Coping with student discipline in school classrooms is an issue in education that just won't go away. For most years since its inception in 1969, the annual Gallup Poll, published in the September issue of *Phi Delta Kappan*, has listed discipline in the schools as the number one problem in the public's perception. According to recent Gallup polls, experienced teachers say student discipline problems are getting worse and significantly interfere with instruction, causing stress so severe that it resembles the battle fatigue of soldiers in combat. As a result, large numbers of beginning teachers leave the teaching profession during or after their first year, reporting that their missionary ideals collapsed when confronted by the rude reality of everyday classroom life.

Many theories address the causes and cures for today's discipline problems. Unfortunately, most people who write and speak about student misconduct are those who have little or no recent classroom experience. Many of the popular commercial materials, designed to prevent and cope with discipline problems, are based on psycho-dynamic theories of behavior and psychiatric anecdotes, not supported by a body of controlled research or extended public school teaching experience.

However, a body of educational research about school discipline does exist. These studies have been published in established professional journals after surviving the scrutiny of independent editorial boards. The studies are often overlooked or dismissed as outdated in the popular educational literature, but are referenced in the **Appendix** because they provide a valid foundation to begin discussing the issue of school discipline. Things may have changed dramatically in education over the last 10 to 20 years, but some solutions may have remained equally effective in coping with student behavior in changed circumstances.

THE CURRENT SITUATION

During the 1990s, educators have seen major changes in children entering elementary schools. Parental neglect due to alcohol and other drug abuse is widespread. Even within relatively intact families, many overworked parents today lack the time or energy to maintain traditional standards of timeliness, spatial rules, respect of property, and reciprocity in relationships—concepts that once contributed greatly to an orderly structure within school classrooms.

To understand and cope better with these major changes, I recently surveyed 60 elementary teachers identified by their principals as highly successful at motivating today's students in both their academic and social behavior. Principals were selected at random in urban and nonurban schools across four central states (Illinois, Wisconsin, Minnesota and Texas).

Follow-up interviews and classroom observations were conducted with 20 of the teachers whose survey responses had the most substantive content.

The survey and interview responses were striking in their recognition of a changed student population, aside from racial or cultural differences. In addition to noting more instances of students arriving at school without an internalized set of behavioral standards or social skills, the respondants reported an increase in students now coming to school without intellectual curiosity or internalized motivation to learn basic academic skills.

Successful teachers indicate that many more students today suffer from attention deficits and are unable to maintain eye contact with the teacher for more than a few seconds or sustain their attention to written work for more than a few minutes at a time. Successful teachers also talk and write extensively about the necessity of making emotional connections with their students and sense a need to reconsider their affective style and the affective climate of their classrooms.

Whether public schools can compensate for what appears to be declining family, neighborhood and church influence is a question and a challenge facing educators today. I am encouraged by the significant number of public school teachers who have been sufficiently perceptive and flexible enough to adapt to the changed needs of their students—and by their principals who recognize their success.

ORGANIZATION OF THIS BOOKLET

This compact volume incorporates practical advice from 60 teachers who participated in the survey (the ones who agreed to allow their names to be published are listed on page 4). This checklist is organized to provide strategies that can help take you through the school year from beginning to end.

Beginning the School Year focuses on how to establish classroom rules and expectations, a positive learning environment, and routines—all of which should minimize behavior problems. It also identifies the kinds of instructional strategies teachers can use that will keep students engaged, on-task, and well-behaved.

Surviving the School Year offers strategies to help you maintain the positive atmosphere you set at the start. Putting a great deal of energy into how you present your lessons, establishing signals that let students know when it's time to focus on work, reinforcing positive behavior and correcting negative behavior, and establishing a positive emotional tone in your classroom can all help curb disciplinary problems.

Because research suggests that **Developing Social Skills** can improve student behavior, this section addresses how to teach students the appropriate ways to treat you and each other, including how to handle difficult situations.

Intervening Flexibly is based on the notion that teachers should react to different types of classroom disruption differently, and suggests what types of intervention are appropriate for specific situations.

In the **Summary and Self-Evaluation Checklist** section, you can see where you stand when it comes to developing better ways of dealing with discipline problems.

The **Appendix** presents an overview of the research on discipline.

WHO CAN BENEFIT FROM THIS CHECKLIST?

With its focus on how to head off discipline problems before they become problems, this checklist can help teachers and other school employees who work directly with children in the classroom deal more effectively with the kinds of behavior that all too frequently disrupt classes and interrupt learning. It can help both the new teacher, who is at-risk of leaving the profession, and the veteran teacher who is struggling with today's difficult students. For both groups, this checklist can demystify how to solve discipline problems, and help you and your students stay focused on learning.

Successful teachers pack a lot of structure into the first day of school. They establish routines and expectations—both behavioral academic—taking into account external contingencies, and do not appear at all concerned about whether they might be perceived as undemocratic, authoritarian or undignified. Although the process of developing rules and expectations may include student suggestions, the successful teachers surveyed had rules and expectations that were mostly predetermined.

CLASSROOM STRUCTURE

Creating a safe learning environment requires that you clearly identify rules and expectations. Almost all successful teachers say the most important thing they do on the first day of school is establish their classroom rules and expectations. Some teachers plan them in advance, while others prefer to develop them collaboratively with their students. Whichever path you take, you will need to teach the rules just as you would teach any other content area. Once the rules are identified and taught, be sure to identify incentives that support them. Preparation includes the following tasks:

1 **Review other teachers' lists of rules and expectations.** Whether you are going to prepare classroom rules ahead of time, or develop them with your class, this is a good first step. Most are simply listed in positive behavioral terms, but some successful teachers combine positive expectations with explicit sanctions. Some examples follow.

Students should:

- look at and listen to the teacher
- play nicely
- speak with indoor voices
- complete work on time
- listen to others
- follow teacher directions
- keep hands, feet, and objects to self
- use a 6-inch (quiet) voice when working
- walk quietly in the halls and room
- raise a hand when you want to speak
- wait your turn
- keep your body in your own space
- work hard
- finish your work carefully

Classroom Rules:

- ▶Treat others with respect
- ▶No teasing, swearing, or put-downs
- ▶Do not interrupt others
- ▶Respect other people's property and space
- ▶Don't touch, push or, hit others
- ▶Stay out of other students' and teachers' desks and storage areas
- ▶Return items that are borrowed
- ▶Respect everyone's right to learn
- ▶Keep voices and noise levels low
- ▶Help others if you can
- ▶Be a good sport

I have the right:

- ▶To be happy and be treated with compassion in this room. This means no one will laugh at me or hurt my feelings.
- ▶To be myself in this room. This means that no one will treat me unfairly because I am black or white, thin or fat, tall or short, boy or girl.
- ▶To be safe in this room. This means that no one will hit me, kick me, push me, pinch me, or hurt me in any way.
- ▶To hear and be heard in this room. This means that no one will yell, scream, shout, or make loud noises.

2 **Decide on a limited number of rules and expectations.** Keep the number small—between five and nine expectations—so your students won't feel overwhelmed. A small number of well-stated, succinct rules will be easier for them to manage, and make it more possible for them to succeed at the behaviors you expect of them.

3 **When making rules collaboratively,** have students brainstorm the kinds of rules that would help them feel safe and make the classroom a place where they can learn. Help them:

- group their suggestions and identify categories of rules;
- consolidate their suggestions to eliminate repetition;
- choose the wording that best conveys their rules and expectations; and
- keep the number of rules small, so students will be able to manage them.

4 **Make a poster of your classroom rules and expectations.** Find wall space where it can remain all year. Leave room on the poster for several additional items that might be suggested by students.

5 **Plan how you will teach the classroom rules and expectations** on the first day and throughout the year. Decide:

- How to begin a class discussion on why schools and classrooms need to have rules that limit student behavior.
- What illustrations on the poster might be helpful.
- What specific examples of acceptable and unacceptable behavior should be presented.
- How the rules and expectations can be reviewed weekly.

6 **List consequences.** Review the following list of consequences that successful teachers use to discourage unsafe or disruptive student behavior. Circle those you would be comfortable discussing the first day of school.

- Separation from a group or work station within classroom
- Minutes subtracted from recess period
- Minutes of after-school detention
- Loss of morning snack (if routinely offered)
- Note or phone call to the parent

7 **List privileges**. Review the following list of privileges that successful teachers use to motivate academic effort of the whole class, and circle those you think would be most appropriate at your grade level.

- End-of-week game time (length determined by points earned)
- Pizza party (scheduled when predetermined number of points earned)
- Popcorn party (depending on when class fills the jar with kernels)
- Lunch in the room with teacher and classmates (dessert provided)
- Afternoon music during seat-work time
- Extra recess time

The structure you introduce at the beginning of the year will help both you and your students feel more comfortable, because you will all know what is expected of you from the start. Identifying the expectations that are most important to maintaining discipline in your classroom, teaching these expectations effectively, and letting students know how they will be rewarded or punished for their behavior sets the proper tone for the year. If we want students to behave well, we have to let them know what good behavior is!

CLASSROOM CLIMATE

Many teachers emphasize the increasing necessity of beginning to establish a positive emotional climate within the classroom the very first day. Rules and consequences provide a necessary safety component to the classroom climate. With today's students, however, it becomes absolutely necessary to establish emotional connections with students, while at the same time maintaining a business-like demeanor. Consider the following strategies recommended by successful teachers:

1 **Spend time evaluating the appearance of your room.** What could you add to make it feel warm, magical, and bright. Would a plant or small lamp on a work table in a corner help? Notice what other teachers do to add warmth to their classrooms.

2 **Think of analogies between classrooms and athletic teams, frontier families, or businesses.** Make it clear than in these groups everyone has to get along with each other without arguing and fighting, everyone has to work hard, and everyone has to care about each other in order to win, survive, or make the group successful.

3 **Consider adopting or creating a class identity, slogan, or logo.** These can foster a sense of belonging and feelings of loyalty to you, to the other students, and to the learning you are undertaking together.

4 **Prepare a short speech about the importance of mutual respect.** What does this mean in terms of behavior? How do respectful teachers talk to students? How can students talk respectfully to each other? How should students talk to teachers? Use some examples of respectful and disrespectful behavior. Stress that treating people with respect will be very important to them throughout their lives.

5 **Find or invent a game to familiarize everyone with students' names.** The sooner students know each other, the more friendly and family-like your class will become. The bonds that students form with each other encourage them to respect each other, and to behave accordingly.

6 **Prepare a short speech in which you share your enthusiasm with students.** Let them know how much you love teaching, how excited and nervous you are about meeting everyone, how much you look forward to getting to know everyone, how important each student's learning is to you, and how much you want them to feel comfortable in your room and have a great year.

7 **Decide what kinds of personal information about yourself and your family you can comfortably share the first day of school.** Sharing some information makes you more human to the students, and will help them see you as someone they will want to respect. But knowing ahead of time what you're willing to tell them and what you want to keep private can prevent awkward moments with your class.

8 **Think of something funny that happened to you during the summer, or sometime in your life, that you can share with students the first day of school.** When you show that you can laugh at yourself, you create a climate where students feel comfortable about making mistakes—which is, after all, an important part of learning!

9 **Prepare a short speech about how to balance hard work with having fun in your classroom.** If your students know that both work and play are going to happen in school, they will know you are concerned with them as people, not only as students. They will also be willing to work at work time, knowing that down time will follow.

10 **Play a fun game at the end of the day.** It's a good way to relax, and enjoy each others' company.

ROUTINES

First day activities must include introducing classroom routines. Routines let you and your students know what to expect regarding day-to-day matters. When students know what's expected of them, they calm down and can more easily maintain good learning behavior. Routines help everyone—including you—get with the program. In developing your classroom routines, think about what makes sense for you, and ask other teachers what procedures they use. Some common classroom routines are:

- ▶Where to store coats and bags.
- ▶Where to put notes from home, lunch money, lunches.
- ▶Using the bathroom and drinking fountains.
- ▶Sharpening pencils.
- ▶Lining up to go to other classrooms, recesses, and lunch.
- ▶Returning from other classrooms and recesses.
- ▶Signals for getting student attention.
- ▶Playground rules.
- ▶Moving about the room during class.
- ▶Handing in and storing written assignments.
- ▶Dismissal procedures for walkers, getting bus riders on correct bus.

Some of these routines you can customize for your classroom; others will need to conform to school-wide policies. In either case, the more you can make routines of daily activities, the less chance students have to develop discipline problems.

INSTRUCTIONAL STRATEGIES

Successful teachers stress the importance of getting right to work and filling the first day with exciting academic activities. You'll want to engage students in a variety of different kinds of activities, so they'll find work interesting and won't feel the urge to create trouble. The more lively, interactive, and challenging the activities, the less likely you'll have discipline problems. Here are some frequently mentioned first-day suggestions.

1 **Include at least one academic task that enables ALL students to succeed.** It's important to get off on the right foot, with every student in your class knowing that he or she will be able to achieve in your class.

2 **Include at least one academic task that will challenge your top students.** This will keep these students involved, and should help other students stretch—and achieve at higher levels.

3 **Begin reading an exciting book to the class.** Let students know that you'll be reading additional installments on a regular basis.

4 **Begin a science project alluding to future "hands-on" activities.** Students who are doing, rather than simply listening, will have fun learning, look forward to new activities—and stay out of trouble!

5 **Make work relevant.** Make sure students know how the work will help them in their "real lives." Prepare a brief rationale for why students should invest effort in learning basic math, spelling, and writing skills. Present this rationale in various forms just before introducing a unit of work.

6 **Begin a portfolio file of monthly writing samples, self-portraits, and other drawings.** Portfolios let students chart their own progress, which can be a big incentive for them to stay interested and keep working hard.

7 **Be sure students take home something new they learned to read or something new they learned that would be of interest to their parents or friends.** Seeing some immediate, tangible results of their work can be a big motivator for students.

8 **Spend some time "hyping" future instructional units.** Students who are looking forward to a new project are less likely to create problems in your classroom.

In a nutshell, when you use creative instructional strategies, your students will have less time and energy to get into trouble. When you stay on your toes, you'll keep them on theirs, too. And the sooner you get started, the better.

Successful teachers today continue to demonstrate the necessity of ongoing vigilance and immediate and consistent follow-through. Verbal approval for appropriate behavior is the most frequent reinforcement. Successful teachers also recommend a variety of more tangible rewards and privileges. Often these reinforcements are offered on a group contingency basis, deliberately using peer pressure to promote behavioral and social standards.

INSTRUCTIONAL PLANNING

Effective instructional planning is the key to motivating students' academic growth. Successful teachers say it matters how a lesson is introduced, how meaningful the content appears to students, the pace at which information is imparted, the amount of variety introduced, and the amount of student involvement. Here are some suggestions for how to meet these challenges throughout the school year.

1 **Think of ways to advertise coming curricular attractions a week or two in advance.** A little "sales pitch" can go a long way toward generating student enthusiasm.

2 **Use songs, poems, or experience-based stories to begin a lesson.** This kind of introduction invites students in to the lesson, letting them know it will be fun and relevant to their lives.

3 **Think of ways to use visual props with your spoken directions.** Visuals can "hook" students into a lesson, and keep them interested and on-task. They will also be sure to attract the attention of students whose preferred learning style is visual.

4 **Vary the presentation of informational material between lecture, video, discussion, and games.** Changes of format keep lessons moving, and students interested.

5 **Experiment with quick, random calling on students instead of waiting for hands during a discussion.** This should keep students on their toes and attentive.

6 **Try talking at different speeds and volumes when you give directions or present information.** See which work best at keeping student interest by evaluating the number of students with their eyes focused on you.

7 **Insist that all students look at you when you give directions.** If a few students begin looking somewhere else in the room, pause and wait for them to give you their full attention.

8 **Use a variety of colored chalk when writing directions or giving information on the chalkboard.** Making the presentation appealing is as important in a classroom as it is in a restaurant. The more attractive the package, the more likely students will want to see what's inside.

9 **Ask the class often if they remember each step in a series of directions you've given.** This encourages their ongoing attention to your instructions. It also gives you the chance to keep students on track, where they'll be less likely to tune out the lesson and distract others.

10 **Have a variety of work stations for some students to complete written work.** Allowing them to move around from station to station burns off physical energy, and doing a variety of work tasks keeps them from getting bored.

11 **Vary the seating chart more than once a month.** Familiarity can lull students into not paying attention. Seeing the classroom from a new seat can keep them fresh.

12 **Be sure each week includes some form of "hands-on" project.** Students learn best when they're "doing," and students who are learning will cause fewer disruptions than those who are bored.

13 **Establish the relevance of your lessons.** With basic academic areas such as math and spelling, think of ways you can begin the lesson by explaining how it is pertinent to an athletic or recreational activity students care about, or to some later life skill or lucrative occupation.

14 **Ask the class often if they understand what they are being asked to do and why they are being asked to do it.** You can defuse potential problems by asking students "Who cares?" before they have a chance to—and then insisting that *they* answer the question!

15 **Limit your help to an individual student to less than a minute,** keeping one eye on the rest of the class. This won't give other students a chance to become disruptive.

16 **Let students know in advance that any recitations must be very short.** Students tend to get distracted when they listen to long student presentations. If other students aren't paying attention, cut the talk short.

17 **Try to break up written work periods during the day so that none is longer than 20 minutes.** Remember, the research shows that too long a time on independent tasks can lead to discipline problems.

18 **Count down the last five minutes of a seat-work period, reminding students of the expected results.** Students will stay on task when they know they'll be held accountable for a finished product at a given time.

19 **Be sure that all materials for the day are organized and ready for quick distribution.** If you're distracted and flipping through papers, students are more likely to get rowdy—so be in your top form!

20 **Mentally rate the interest level of your lessons on a 10-point scale** and make a note of those with a rating of seven or above. See if you can accumulate enough 7^+ lessons to fill the school year.

21 **Ask other teachers what they taught last week that seemed to pique the interest of their students the most.** Getting ideas from other professionals can keep you fresh and keep your students engaged and learning.

Implementing these suggestions will improve your ability to reach your students, and the more you can reach them, the fewer discipline problems you're going to have.

SIGNALING/CUEING

Survey responses show that the various signals successful teachers use to get and hold students' attention to directions, information, and tasks are considered an important part of getting students motivated. The following list of recommendations can help you accomplish these goals.

1 **Getting students' attention.** Review the following list of what teachers say to get students to listen to their directions and circle those that seem most applicable to your grade level and personal style.

- I need to see everyone's eyes looking at me.
- 1, 2, 3. Eyes on me.
- When I see everyone's eyes, I'll know you're ready to begin.
- Stop, look and (in unison) listen.
- Eyes on me, ears listening, mouth closed, feet quiet, seat on rug.

2 **Get students back on task.** Memorize at least three of the following questions teachers ask to redirect student attention to the assigned task.

- Are you with me?
- Can I help?
- Having trouble?
- Are you doing your job?
- Can you repeat my directions?

3 **Review other ways teachers get or redirect student attention to the assigned task.** Circle those that appear most appropriate for your grade level and personal style.

- Counting forwards or backwards from five.
- Beginning a rhythmic clap that the students finish or imitate.

- ▶Giving a particular student "The Eye" (an intense stare with head tilted and one eyebrow raised).
- ▶Raising one hand with outstretched fingers and saying, "Give me five" (each finger representing a listening or working expectation).
- ▶"Excuse me!"
- ▶"I want to see everyone seated, lips closed, bodies quiet."
- ▶"Mouth! Chair! Hands! Eyes!"
- ▶ "This is your first and last warning" (of impending consequences).

4 **Rate yourself.** On a 10-point scale, score your behavior on the following kinds of body language successful teachers commonly associate with on-task student behavior. Ask a colleague to swap observational ratings on the same items.

- ▶Displays confident body posture (e.g., standing tall, feet planted solidly on the ground).
- ▶Uses a strong voice.
- ▶Moves vigorously around the room.
- ▶Uses many hand and facial gestures of approval and disapproval.
- ▶Is highly vigilant, constantly scanning the room.
- ▶Shows energetic and enthusiastic facial expressions.

When students become familiar with your signals that you want their attention, you will be able to quickly draw their focus to you, and minimize behavioral problems.

REINFORCEMENT TECHNIQUES

All of the successful teachers surveyed and interviewed referred to the necessity of reinforcing their expectations and rules with rewards and punishments. Frequent use of verbal approval is the most common reward mentioned. A surprising number of successful teachers also mention their regular use of concrete reinforcements and privileges to motivate student effort. All of the teachers, however, stress the need to respond immediately to unsafe or disruptive student behavior with unpleasant negative consequences.

1 **Review the following list of words and phrases** successful teachers use to motivate academic effort and circle those you think would be most appreciated by students who have difficulty achieving at an average rate.

- ▶You did that just right.
- ▶You are such good listeners.
- ▶That's well thought out.
- ▶You have a good head on you today.
- ▶Jolly good answer.
- ▶You are showing improvement.
- ▶That is certainly so.
- ▶That's such a good paper.
- ▶Well, I should say so.
- ▶You can be proud of yourself.
- ▶Right you are.
- ▶Now you're cooking.
- ▶Good progress
- ▶You're on the right track.
- ▶I'm pleased.
- ▶I like the way you're working.
- ▶How about that!
- ▶You are a careful thinker.

- Excellent answer.
- I knew you could do that well.
- That's right.
- That's what I call being observant.
- This is the greatest.
- Wow! Better than ever. You're working especially well.
- Very conscientious.
- You couldn't have said it better.
- Great!
- You've been listening with both ears.
- Beautiful!
- Please repeat. That's worth hearing twice.
- Stupendous!
- I'm glad to see you working in your seat here.
- Perfect!
- You're putting some good effort into this.
- Fantastic!
- Susie has her thinking cap on today.
- That answer has the rest of us thinking now.
- Bravo!
- We accomplished a lot today.
- Wonderful!
- Say, you're on the ball.
- Splendid!
- It feels good to come into such a good class.
- Lovely!
- Everyone seems to like that answer.
- Superb!
- Cool!
- This is result of hard work by every one of you.
- Much better!
- You're getting better at finishing the assignments.
- Marvelous!

- ▶Your good study habits are helping you get a lot done.
- ▶Good work!
- ▶Anyone would love to work with this group.

2 **Compliment student effort.** Identify and memorize at least five new ways each month of the year. Sincere expressions of your approval can work wonders keeping students motivated.

3 **Review a portfolio of each student's work once a month.** Record and communicate their area of greatest improvement. Students thrive when they see concrete samples of their progress.

4 **Review the following list of privileges and concrete reinforcements** that successful teachers use to motivate the whole class's academic effort, and circle those you think would be most appropriate at your grade level.

- ▶End-of-day socializing time (2–10 minutes depending on behavior)
- ▶Class award posters
- ▶Class sticker posters
- ▶Extra videotape
- ▶Free reading time
- ▶Marbles in a jar for privilege time

5 **Review the following list of unpleasant consequences** that successful teachers use to discourage the repetition of unsafe or disruptive student behavior after only one warning. Rank those you use or plan to use before referring an individual student to the school principal.

- ▶1–5 minute separation from a group within the classroom
- ▶1–5 minute isolation in a time-out station within the classroom
- ▶1–5 minutes subtracted from recess period
- ▶5–15 minutes subtracted from recess period

- 5–30 minutes in a quiet detention room within the school
- 5–30 minutes after-school detention
- loss of morning snack (if routinely offered)
- note or phone call to the parent

Be prepared to praise your students generously when they're doing well—it will encourage them to continue to excel. But also be prepared to stop your students when they're misbehaving. Taking away privileges, having them make up missed time after school or during recess, or contacting a parent all encourage students to behave well in class.

AFFECTIVE STRATEGIES

Affective strategies—those that create an emotional bond with students—that you initiate the first day need to be extended throughout the school year. Successful teachers recommend the following ways to do this.

1 **Look for inspirational materials, music, stories, poetry or videos you can use to elicit positive emotional responses from students.** When students are inspired, they will work hard to achieve their goals, and will present fewer discipline problems because they will be fully engaged in learning.

2 **Schedule time near the end of each day to reflect and discuss the day's interpersonal interactions, and how students feel about them**. In what ways do students feel teachers did or did not respect their feelings? How did students show—or fail to show—respect for the feelings of other students? How did students show—or fail to show—respect for their teachers? Help students develop their problem-solving skills by exploring alternative ways to interact.

3 **Schedule a daily or weekly journal writing time** when students can write private letters to the teacher and receive written teacher responses. These interactions help create a feeling of safety for

students, who can trust that you care about how they're feeling about what's going on in the classroom. Students who feel attended to often forego disruptive attention-getting behaviors.

4 **Introduce the concept of self-effacing humor with personal examples.** Schedule a weekly time when students can volunteer to read or narrate a "most embarrassing moment," real or fictional. The aim of these disclosures is for everyone to feel comfortable being themselves.

Review Your Class List

5 **Note the ways some students have contributed to a positive classroom climate.** Sharing these examples with the class communicates that you believe classroom climate is as important as the subject matter you are studying. Repeat monthly.

- Note how some students have made you laugh or cry the last month. Share these experiences with a friend or family member. When you take care of yourself, you won't take your frustrations out on your students with anger and impatience.
- Note what each child prides the most in his or her life. Acknowledge the source of the child's pride, and encourage the children to develop the attributes and skills they're proud of.
- Develop a monthly plan for building stronger relationships with two students. Students will appreciate your attention.
- Devise a plan for improving your knowledge of the home life of two of your students. Students often come to school with concerns that get in the way of learning. Knowing about these can help you help them, so they can focus fully on learning.

6 **Rehearse a daily greeting that is unique and related to some special interest or talent of each student.** Students who feel special, and who get your attention for their strengths, are less likely to misbehave.

Students are whole people. Interacting with them on an emotional as well as an intellectual level—within appropriate bounds—leads them to feel more comfortable, more trusting, and more able to learn.

Developing or purchasing a curricular scope and sequence of social skills is seen as an important beginning point. Explicit expectations and direct instruction are also necessary. But the most important aspect of teaching social skills is the demonstration and practice of socially appropriate language and behavior via role-playing, acting out short skits and emulating positive role models in our society.

COMMUNICATING EXPECTATIONS

As discussed in the introduction, today's students are different from students in the past. More of them are coming from homes where parents are overworked and have much less time to spend with them. As a result, more children come to school less socialized than students of earlier generations. Part of your job, then, becomes helping these children learn appropriate ways of behaving with others. Consider the following ways teachers make their social expectations more explicit.

1 **Review the list of rules and expectations you introduced the first day of school and identify which address safety, disruptive behavior, and social issues.** Based on the social interaction problems experienced by students as the year progresses, add appropriate social expectations—such as asking for information or to join an activity, apologizing, dealing effectively with conflict—and review them with the class.

2 **Begin a "Chart of Cooperation."** List a few examples of how some students have helped others or contributed something to the class. Add other examples weekly as you or students notice them occurring.

3 **Prepare a "Good Manners" bulletin board with a number of examples.** Begin a discussion of additional items.

4 **Develop a "Bill of Students' Rights."** In conjunction with an early American History unit on the United States Constitution, divide the class into three or four committees. This will help students learn the lesson at hand, and also validate the importance of their own rights with respect to social interaction in the classroom.

5 **Prepare a lesson on empathy.** Include many examples of treating others as you would like to be treated, caring, respecting others' feelings, and putting yourself in the other person's shoes.

6 **Review the following social skill expectations** and indicate which you wish to address at different times during the school year.

- ▶Beginning a conversation
- ▶Joining in a game
- ▶Asking a favor
- ▶Offering help to a classmate
- ▶Suggesting an activity
- ▶Sharing
- ▶Apologizing
- ▶Responding to teasing
- ▶Staying out of fights
- ▶Dealing with an accusation
- ▶Dealing with boredom
- ▶Identifying and understanding what caused a problem
- ▶Making a complaint
- ▶Answering a complaint
- ▶Dealing with losing
- ▶Dealing with being left out
- ▶Dealing with group pressure

7 **Keep parents informed, and get their help.** In a newsletter to parents, include a section on what social skill objectives you have emphasized last month and those you plan to emphasize the coming month.

Clearly defining what you expect from students in terms of social skills makes it possible for you to teach these skills, and for students to succeed in developing them. The following sections of this chapter deal with how to teach social skills in your classroom.

MODELING POSITIVE INTERACTIONS

Successful teachers make a point of reporting that just telling students what's expected doesn't get it to happen. This is particularly true in the area of developing social skills. To surmount a wide range of negative role models on television, in movie theaters, and even within the home and neighborhood, you must find fictional, historical, and current day characters that promote the values and social skills of a civilized society. Then you must teach students to role play positive scenarios on an ongoing basis. Consider which of the following approaches would work best for you.

1 **Ask your school librarian for a list of books, stories, and videos that present positive role models for children.** Make these available to your students.

2 **Prepare a "Hero Book Rack" for materials you have borrowed or purchased.** Include sports heroes. Allow students to browse if they finish their written work early.

3 **Visit your librarian and find out how to locate news stories on heroic feats.** When you find these stories, share them with your class.

4 **Collect back issues of *Time* and copy or tear out the Local Hero of the Week section.** Tack them up on a poster board and have the students vote on their favorite. Have groups of students campaign for their choice.

5 **Have students who are sports-minded nominate an athlete for the "Most Sportsmanlike Conduct" of the week.** Emphasize qualities such as getting along with others, being a good winner or loser, and being a team player. Let students defend and debate their choice among competing nominations.

6 **Use journals.** Have students write or draw pictures in their journal on assigned topics such as friendship, trust, respect, bullying, name calling, etc.

7 **Use role playing.** Collaborate with another teacher, spouse, or friend to role play or act out common school conflict situations such as name calling, mother name calling, line budging, accidental bumping, or tripping. Present smart and dumb ways of dealing with conflicts. Involve students in scripting smarter ways of dealing with social problems.

8 **Have students role play destructive and constructive language in various social situations.** Some examples are: including oneself in a play activity, competing for friendships, dealing with criticisms, "put-downs," etc.

9 **Have students practice kindness, fairness, and caring phrases in little skits for the class.** Practice makes perfect!

10 **Praise kindness.** Look for students who include others in their play or activity on the playground, and praise them publicly when you have observed two or three such examples.

Giving students a chance to see role models and positive interactions can open up a new world of possible ways to behave with others. Giving them a chance to practice interacting constructively can stop problems before they start.

DISCUSSING PROBLEM SITUATIONS

Successful teachers say they must use some instructional time to discuss social problem situations. Unresolved, these problem situations can sometimes fester, involving more students and making it extremely difficult to motivate academic attention and effort.

Consider which of the following ways you might begin to resolve problem situations.

1 **Discussing problems.** Set aside 5 minutes of show-and-tell time at the primary grade levels to discuss possible solutions to real or fictional problems in social interactions on the playground.

2 **Create a sealed "Social Problems Box."** Students can anonymously submit observations of social problems in their classroom. Deal with these at a regularly scheduled weekly time.

3 **Review and memorize the following questions teachers ask** when attempting to resolve social conflict.

- Tell me what he or she did to start the problem.
- What did you do to try to fix the problem?
- Did that help?
- Did that make it better or worse?
- Would you do that again?
- What can you do when you are angry?
- What will you do the next time this happens?
- What would you like to say to ______ to make things better?

4 **Teach students the value of using "I" messages.** It's possible to defuse a conflict situation by saying, "I'm angry that I wasn't included in your game," instead of saying "You're a jerk for not inviting me." "I" messages teach children to take responsibility for their own feelings, rather than blaming others, and other people are more receptive to hearing "I" messages rather than being accused of something.

5 **Become familiar with the following conflict resolution procedure.** Use it outside of instructional time when two students have conflicts on a repetitive basis.

- Ask Child #1 to state the problem and how he felt about it. Instruct Child #2 to listen to what

Child #1 is saying, because she will have to repeat what the other person said.

- Ask Child #2 to repeat what Child #1 said.
- Reverse the process with Child # 2 stating what she thinks the problem is and how she felt about it and Child #1 repeating what Child # 2 said.
- Ask both children what they need to do to get along better. (Brainstorm solutions.)
- Decide which solutions to support or impose.

Conflict resolution techniques can keep small disagreements small. When students learn to communicate effectively even when they disagree, they are less likely to be part of discipline problems.

USING CURRICULAR MATERIALS

Many of the successful teachers surveyed and interviewed reported that their schools had recently adopted a commercial social skills curriculum. Without this structure of materials and regular use, the teachers say such things as "I would be lost," or "I wouldn't get any real teaching done."

Ask your principal, district curriculum consultant or librarian which of the following materials or other materials are or could be made available on loan for your review.

- *Second Step: A Violence-Prevention Curriculum*
  by Kathy Beland
  Committee for Children
  2203 Airport Way South, Suite 500
  Seattle, Washington 98134-2027
  (800) 634-4449

- *Skill-Streaming the Elementary School Child*
  by Ellen McGinnis and Arnold P. Goldstein
  Research Press Company
  Dept. 171, P.O. Box 9177
  Champaign, Illinois 61821
  (217) 352-3273

- *Ready-to-Use Social Skills Lessons and Activities,* by Ruth Weltmann Begun
  The Society for Prevention of Violence with
  The Center for Applied Research in Education
  Prentice Hall Career and Personal Development
  113 Sylvan Avenue
  Englewood Cliffs, NJ 07632

- *Bullyproof: A Teachers Guide on Teasing and Bullying for use with Fourth and Fifth Grade Students*, by Lisa Sjostrom and Nan Stein
  NEA Professional Library
  P.O. Box 2035
  Annapolis Junction, MD 20701
  (800) 229-4200

- *Quit It! A Teachers Guide on Teasing and Bullying for use with Students in Grades K–3*
  by Merle Froschl, Barbara Sprung, Nancy Mullin-Rindler, Nan Stein, and Nancy Gropper
  NEA Professional Library
  P.O. Box 2035
  Annapolis Junction, MD 20701
  (800) 229-4200

INTERVENING FLEXIBLY

When successful teachers were asked to select personal characteristics that best described them, the most common responses were "organized" and "flexible." Their organizational skills are evident in their preparation for teaching social behaviors along with academic subjects. Flexibility is evident in the way they approach different kinds of problem behaviors in different ways.

TRANSITIONS

School staff experience their most difficult time with student behavior during transitions. As students change from one activity to another, return from recess or a special event, or move from one part of the room to another, successful teachers report the necessity of using a number of strategies. Consider the following.

1 **As you announce an upcoming transition, remind students of the kind of behavior you're looking for.** Restate your expectation of moving quietly and slowly without bumping, shoving, or touching others with hands or feet.

2 **Publicly compliment those groups of students complying with your transition expectations.** Say such things as, "I like the way John, Sue and Paul are moving quietly to their seats. Some of you, I see, are already sitting ready to begin. OK, now I see more of you are ready to go to work."

3 **As students reenter the classroom, have the next activity waiting for them.** Put a message on the overhead projector about how to get ready for the next lesson, or have an assignment or the seatwork for a lesson already distributed on their desk.

4 **After all students have reentered the room, give a signal that you are ready to begin.** Say, "Let's get started," or "We have much work to do," or "The sooner we can begin, the sooner we can finish," or turn off the lights, count backwards from 5 or ring a small bell. Then look at the clock, set a timer or raise fingers on your hand with the prearranged understanding that lost minutes of instruction will be made up by the whole class (or a few individuals) before leaving for recess or lunch.

5 **If you have trouble getting students to settle down, remind them of the consequences of their choices.** Print the word "RECESS" on the chalkboard as a warning and remove one letter for each 5 seconds of lost instructional time,

or tell students, "If you need to use my time now, I will need a bit more of your time at lunch or recess."

6 **Keep students focused on the next activity.** Intently whisper what comes next, making it sound too inviting to want to miss.

7 **Avoid redirecting individuals, repeatedly reprimanding the class generally or pleading for student attention and compliance.** If the transition time takes too long, sit down, take a deep breath and quietly go over the rules and consequences and then try the transition in the room again.

When you have different methods for making transitions smoothly, you minimize the chance that students will behave disruptively at these times. Try out some of the ideas listed above, and see which ones you feel most comfortable with. Remember, transition time need not be traumatic!

CLOWNING

Teachers see clowning as an inappropriate attention-getting device that unfortunately is successful much of the time for the attention-seeking student. To deal with such behavior, consider which of the following you would or wouldn't do.

1 **Avoid public reprimands of a student clowning; instead, try one of these responses:**

- Move toward a clowning student without making eye contact.
- Give a private warning of impending isolation from the group within the classroom.
- Isolate the clowning student to the rear of the classroom for a short time (1–5 min.) after only one warning.

2 **For repeated incidents of clowning, schedule a private conference with the student during recess or lunch.** Present rationales for doing the clowning outside of the classroom and discuss alternative ways of getting attention (class plays, show-and-tell time, or a few minutes of stand-up comedy at the end of the day).

3 **Make a written signed contract for improving behavior.** Include incentives and the possibility of being excluded from fun activities if the clowning continues.

4 **Enlist class support in ignoring a student's inappropriate bid for attention.** Say, "Please don't pay attention to his/her nonsense. We're in school and we have quite a bit to do—don't let ________ steal your time."

REFUSALS

When students refuse to attempt a written assignment, successful teachers usually begin by offering several forms of assistance, continue by offering various forms of reinforcement and, if necessary, end up reviewing expectations and consequences. If the student refuses to accept any consequences you should consider it extremely serious. You must contact the parents and/or principal for their support in dealing with the child's defiance. Consider using some of the strategies from the following range of suggestions.

1 **Start by offering to help the student.** Try these options.

- Sit with the student, show a caring attitude, and do a few problems together.
- Remind the student of a previous similar assignment that he or she completed successfully.
- Tease the student nicely and privately to find the "start button."
- Ask if the student understands the assignment.

- Suggest that the student skip the first problem and pick another for getting started.

2 Look for possible reasons the student might be having trouble, and respond appropriately.

- If the work-refusal problem is recent, call the parents to ask if they know what could be upsetting their child at school.
- In the case of a possible learning disability, modify the assignment.

3 Offer encouragement and positive reinforcement for efforts made.

- Express verbal approval for any sign of beginning the assignment even if the student just picks up the pencil.
- Communicate high expectations of work effort. Say something like, "Rule #1 in this classroom is that everyone must participate. That's 100 percent. Can't or won't is a bad word we just do not use. At least try first and if you need help, I'll be there."

4 Give the student several choices, letting him or her know that there will be consequences for not participating in the activity.

- "Work now during class time or work during lunch time or after school, or go to the detention room or office and do the work."
- If the problem persists, ask the student if you should make a "hot-call" to the parents asking them to, for example, take away weekend privileges and activities.

When students refuse to work, initiate a sequence of responses that move from positive reinforcement to warning about consequences. Be sure to follow through.

INTERRUPTING

Although interrupting can be extremely irritating, most successful teachers consider this a relatively mild form of misconduct and deal with it accordingly. Consider the range of strategies suggested.

1 In most cases, you can deal with interrupting gently and with humor.

- Remind students that you expect them to raise hands, wait their turn to speak, and be patient.
- Defer interrupting questions and comments to a later time saying, "Wait. Not now. Hang on to that thought."
- Move your hand gently to block eye contact with the interrupting student.
- At the upper grades use humor, saying, "Excuse me, is the middle of my sentence interrupting the beginning of yours?"

2 Most students don't intend to be rude when they interrupt, and you should deal with their behavior by educating them about why it is better to wait their turn.

- With habitually interrupting students, schedule a private conference and describe interrupting as unfair, distracting, and disrespectful of others' feelings and rights. Make a written signed contract to improve their behavior.
- With extremely impulsive children, work out a private hand signal to remind the students of expectations. (Examples: teacher touches top of left ear or ear lobe, holds up two or three fingers, or moves hand or finger down as if making a hash mark.) Have them monitor their own progress by recording "talk-outs" or rating themselves on a 10 point scale daily.

These methods should help students who interrupt learn to change their behavior.

SOCIALIZING

For socializing at inappropriate times, successful teachers usually begin by suggesting a variety of softer approaches and then gradually escalate to more severe measures. Consider the following sequence.

1 Begin by suggesting alternate times when students can socialize without interfering with learning.

- Remind students that they can socialize before or after school, or during lunch and recesses.
- Suggest to chronic socializers that they exchange phone numbers so they can talk to each other at home.

2 Provide time for socializing as a reward earned for good behavior. Allow students to talk quietly to a friend during the last 5–10 minutes of school if the class has earned such a privilege in one-minute increments throughout the day.

3 Reprimand students when necessary, and implement punishments when other methods have failed to stop the behavior.

- Use eye contact to communicate disapproval of inappropriate socializing.
- Isolate the chief offender to a chair at the back of the room away from all students until the lesson is over.
- Assign incomplete work resulting from socializing as homework with parent contact or parent signature required.

Socializing is an important element of your students' day. Your goal isn't to stop it, only to confine it to appropriate times, when it won't interfere with learning.

SUMMARY AND SELF-EVALUATION CHECKLIST

Many of the suggestions from successful teachers are consistent with the body of research on discipline cited in the Appendix. However, many of the suggestions in this book extend the research and sometimes challenge the "collective wisdom" of educators.

BEYOND THE RESEARCH

Consistent with Emmer and Evertson's (1980) results, successful teachers pack a lot of structure into that first day of school.

1 Examples of suggestions in this book that go beyond Emmer and Evertson's research are:

- Successful teachers attempt to establish emotional contact with their students on the very first day.
- Successful teachers put time and effort into establishing a physically positive classroom atmosphere. They also begin sharing personal, affective experiences.
- Depending on the grade level, successful teachers may also introduce the concept of mutual respect and explore with their students the feelings that accompany demonstrations of respect or the lack of respect.
- The emphasis successful teachers give to such affective variables, in addition to their efforts in establishing rules and consequences, provides a more balanced approach to discipline than you will find in much of the scholarly literature.

2 The recommendations in this book:

- Support the research of Kounin (1970) with respect to the necessity of ongoing vigilance and immediate and consistent follow-through. Verbal approval for appropriate behavior is the most frequent reinforcement.
- Extend this research by creating a variety of more tangible rewards and privileges. Often these reinforcements are offered on a group contingency basis, deliberately using peer pressure to promote behavioral and social standards.

- ▶ Support the research of Jones (1979) and others who identified the importance of body language and nonverbal signals to redirect student attention.
- ▶ Extend this and other research by presenting a wide selection of verbal signals as well.

3 Providing nonsatiating, challenging lessons, building variety into learning programs, providing individual help efficiently, and using humor are strategies supported by the research. Because the way units of instruction are introduced becomes critical to their success in capturing interest, successful teachers extend the list of instructional variables to include "advertising" coming curricular attractions, using "hands-on" activities, and preparing rationales for teaching the basics.

4 The **most significant** extension of previous research that emerged from the strategies of teachers who contributed to this book is in the area of teaching social skills. Successful teachers:

- ▶ Developed or purchased a curricular scope and sequence of social skills.
- ▶ Communicated explicit expectations and provided direct instruction on social skills.
- ▶ Demonstrated and practiced socially appropriate language and behavior via role-playing, acting out short skits, and emulating positive role models in our society.

5 Another way that successful teachers expand the research is the way they employ intervention techniques flexibly, depending on the kind of student misconduct encountered.

- ▶ Interrupting, for example, is dealt with at a different level than inappropriate socializing.
- ▶ Clowning receives a somewhat different set of responses than task refusal.
- ▶ Signals and other responses to task refusal are quite different from those used for inappropriate socializing.

- Strategies for dealing with students who do not return to task after recess or a special class involve a much wider span of interventions.

6 Finally, the language successful teachers use to communicate with students brings further specificity to the professional literature. In this book, teachers share the words they use to:

- establish expectations,
- praise small increments of student progress,
- describe the choices students must make about the consequences of their behavior,
- get students' attention,
- offer academic assistance,
- ask questions about their social misconduct, and
- deal humorously with clowning and interrupting.

Beginning teachers who read this book can be confident that the words and phrases offered as suggestions in the text have been tested and proven effective.

SELF-EVALUATION CHECKLIST

After considering the survey responses of successful teachers, along with replicated research results, I have organized all these findings into a 20-item summary checklist. You can use this checklist to rate yourself by identifying your strengths (**S**) and the areas you would like to improve (**I**).

	S	I
Has written rules, expectations, and well thought out procedures that are posted, taught and regularly reviewed.	☐	☐
Visually scans all students frequently and intervenes immediately when expectations are not being met.	☐	☐

	S	I
Gives verbal warnings/choices of impending consequences and follows through.	☐	☐
Uses hand and facial gestures to signal privileges as approval and disapproval.	☐	☐
Uses concrete reinforcements and incentives.	☐	☐
Uses praise, smiles, and other forms of approval frequently and appropriately.	☐	☐
Uses penalties and unpleasant consequences as deterrents.	☐	☐
Uses private conferences to address chronic misconduct.	☐	☐
Gives specific directions for transition periods, monitors closely, and gives frequent feedback.	☐	☐
Makes emotional connections with students.	☐	☐
Shows and demands respect with students.	☐	☐
Makes expectations for social behavior explicit.	☐	☐
Uses positive social role models and role playing.	☐	☐
Follows a sequence of social skills objectives or a curriculum.	☐	☐
Has materials organized and ready for quick distribution.	☐	☐
Provides help efficiently.	☐	☐
Hypes the introduction of lessons.	☐	☐
Limits the length of recitations and seat work activities.	☐	☐
Plans nonsatiating, varied and challenging lessons.	☐	☐
Adapts the level of work difficulty for some students.	☐	☐

Best of luck on your journey toward a well-disciplined, productive classroom, where both you and your students thrive!

APPENDIX: What the Research Says

The research about discipline focuses on two major areas: The first looks at the teacher behaviors—including teaching methods—that encourage good student conduct. The second addresses the ways teachers intervene when student behavior becomes disruptive.

Teacher Behaviors

Kounin is credited with beginning the modern era of research on classroom management in 1970. With an educator's background, he analyzed the videotapes of third grade classrooms. He identified teacher behaviors and teaching strategies that decreased the amount of off-task time and deviancy of students. These included:

- **Vigilance.** Teachers who were highly alert to what was going on in their classrooms were successful in minimizing bad behavior.
- **Multi-tasking.** Effective teachers were able to deal with more than one situation at a time.
- **Rapid response.** Teachers had to be ready to intervene immediately before misbehavior escalated.
- **Smooth transitions.** Careful planning that allowed the class to shift easily from one task to another prevented discipline problems.
- **A whole-group focus.** Keeping the class on track together made it possible to avoid misbehavior.
- **Challenging learning programs.** When students were academically challenged, they were more likely to stay on-task and working.

Kounin and a number of other educational researchers (Good, 1978; Gump, 1969; Bossert, 1977), as well *The Beginning Teacher Evaluation Study* (BTES) identified the teacher behaviors that led to higher levels of student-engagement. These included:

- **Teacher-led Group Settings.** Students were more engaged than during independent seat-work sessions.

- ▶**Teacher Academic Feedback.** Students responded to higher amounts of feedback by remaining involved in their work.
- ▶**More Substantive Instruction.** Teacher signals and control of questions were associated with higher student engagement (Filby, 1978).

Arlin's studies (1979) gave further support to the importance of smooth transitions, first identified by Kounin, showing that when teachers provided closely monitored transitions, with specific directions and frequent feedback, rates of off-task student behavior were significantly reduced. Several of these studies also found that when teachers allowed long periods of student recitation or long periods of contact among students, on-task behaviors throughout the classroom deteriorated.

Perhaps the most startling finding about student discipline was Frederick Jones': that typical classrooms lose approximately 50 percent of their instructional time because students are talking off-task without permission and generally "goofing off." Jones and his associates drew this conclusion after conducting thousands of hours of carefully controlled classroom observations. From observing teachers who were notably successful in dealing with such problems, they formulated three clusters of recommendations about teacher behavior:

- ▶**Body Language.** Teachers who were able to deal effectively with discipline maintained confident postures, vigorous movement, eye contact, facial expression, a strong voice, and nonverbal signals, such as gestures and proximity, to keep their classrooms under control.
- ▶**Incentive Systems.** Teachers who were able to deal effectively with discipline regularly praised and rewarded good behavior, and they also informed students of the negative consequences of inappropriate behavior.
- ▶**Academic Help for Individual Students.** Teachers who were able to deal effectively with discipline were able to keep students on-task by helping those who were having difficulty

with course material before they had a chance to disrupt the class.

Jones also discovered that the characteristic students prized the most in successful teachers was their sense of humor.

This line of research culminated with the work of Emmer and Evertson (1980), who identified teachers who produced higher rates of learning and on-task behavior in third grade classrooms. Effective teacher-managers were distinguished by establishing rules, routines, and interventions as well as by using pedagogical methods that engaged students. Specifically, these teachers:

- established rules and classroom procedures;
- monitored student behavior and intervened immediately with incentives and consequences for positive and negative behavior;
- clearly communicated instructional objectives and directions;
- built variety into the curriculum; and
- organized materials well and distributed them smoothly.

Then, in 1983, Evertson, Emmer, Sanford and Clements carried out an experimental design showing that it was possible to train beginning teachers to become better managers using the strategies found in their correlational research. Stallion and Zimpher (1991) later confirmed the importance of conducting such training at the beginning of the school year.

Intervention Strategies

A second line of research examined how teachers perceived various kinds of intervention strategies. These studies focused more on what strategies were more commonly implemented and why, or why others were not. Algozzine and associates (1983) had teachers rate 40 interventions relative to case study descriptions of an immature child, a child with learning difficulties, and an unmanageable child.

Half of the interventions were ways to transfer responsibility to others—such as a physician, social worker, tutor or special education teacher. The other half involved activities that the teacher could perform more directly. The strategies receiving the highest ratings involved getting consultation and more knowledge from a variety of sources and making instructional modifications.

Johnson and Pugach (1980) asked teachers how often they used 57 intervention strategies and how reasonable these strategies were for implementation with a student showing mild problems with both learning and behavior. Top-ranked interventions were talking about the problem with the parents and other teachers, adjusting performance expectations, verbalizing the student's effort and other good qualities, and providing predetermined incentives for appropriate behavior.

Martens, Peterson, Witt, and Cirone (1986) used a list of intervention strategies to analyze teacher perceptions of effectiveness, ease of use, and frequency of use. They found that teachers considered the most effective and easiest form of intervention to be using various forms of signals redirecting students' behavior. Various ways of manipulating previously contracted material rewards were also rated as highly effective, although not as easy or frequently used. Consultation with various specialists and a "time-out" or removal from the group or classroom were also commonly used, but received less favorable ratings.

Elliot, Witt, Galvin and Peterson (1984) analyzed the acceptability of only three positive and three negative reinforcements for various severe behavior problems. The study found that teachers considered praise and home-based reinforcement significantly more acceptable than token economy interventions, no matter how severe the behavior problem. The researchers also found that a response-cost lottery (removing privileges) was the overwhelming favorite teacher intervention for all three problem behaviors (daydreaming, using obscene language, and destroying others' property).

REFERENCES

Algozzine, B., Ysseldyke, J., Christenson, S. and Thurlow, M. 1983. A factor analysis of teachers' intervention choices for dealing with students' behavior and learning problems. *The Elementary School Journal* 84:43–52.

Arlin, M. 1979. Teacher transitions can disrupt time flow in classrooms. *American Educational Research Journal* 16:42–56.

Bossert, S. 1977. Tasks, group management and teacher control behavior: a study of classroom organization and teacher style. *School Review* 85:552–565.

Elam, S. 1989. The 2nd annual Gallup Phi Delta Kappan poll of teacher attitude towards public schools. *Phi Delta Kappan* 70:785–798.

Elliott, S. Witt, J. Galvin, G. and Peterson, R. 1984. Acceptability of positive and reductive behavioral interventions: Factors that influence teachers' decisions. *Journal of School Psychology* 22:353–360.

Emmer, E., Evertson, C. and Anderson, L. 1980. Effective classroom management at the beginning of the school year. *The Elementary School Journal* 80:219–231.

Evertson, C., Emmer, E., and Clements B. 1983. Improving classroom management: an experiment in elementary classrooms. *The Elementary School Journal* 84:173–189.

Filby, N. 1978. How teachers produce academic learning time: instructional variables related to student engagement. Paper presented at the annual meeting of the American Educational Research Association, Toronto.

Good, T. and Beckerman, T. 1978. Time-on-task: A naturalistic study in sixth-grade classrooms. *The Elementary School Journal* 78:193–201.

Gump, P. 1969. Intra-setting analysis: the third grade classroom as a special but instructive case. *Naturalistic Viewpoints in Psychological Research*, edited by E. Williams and H. Rausch. New York: Rinehart and Winston.

Johnson, L. and Pugach, M. 1990. Classroom teachers' views of intervention strategies for learning and behavior problems: Which are reasonable and how frequently are they used? *The Journal of Special Education* 24:69–84.

Jones, F. 1979. The gentle art of classroom discipline. *National Elementary Principal* 58:26–32.

Kounin, J. 1970. *Discipline and group management in classrooms.* New York: Holt, Rinehart & Winston.

Martens, B., Peterson, R., Witt, J. and Cirone, S. 1986. Teacher perceptions of school-based interventions. *Exceptional Children* 53:213–223.

Smith, M. and Misra, A. 1992. A comprehensive management system for students in regular classrooms. *The Elementary School Journal* 92:353–371.

Stallion, L. and Zimpher, L. 1991. Classroom management and intervention: The effects of training and mentoring on the inductive teacher's behavior. *Action In Teacher Education* 13:42–50.

Veen, S. 1984. Perceived problems of beginning teachers. *Review of Educational Research* 54:143–178.

Wolfgang, C. and Kelsay, K. 1991. Discipline and today's students: They're sure not what they used to be! *Contemporary Education* 62:150–155.